Practice Tests for Math GOAL 2 Level E, Forms 929M and 930M

Helping Learners Develop Mathematical Thinking Skills, Approach Math with Confidence, and Sharpen their Test-Taking Ability

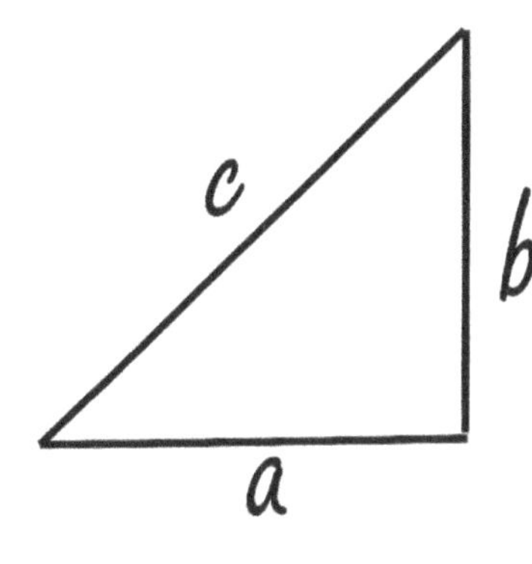

By

CBL COACHING
FOR BETTER LEARNING

TABLE OF CONTENTS

Dear Instructors,

This book entails four (4) practice tests and is designed to prepare adult learners for the CASAS Math GOALS 2, Level E Forms 929M and 930M. The practice tests align with the CASAS Competencies and meet the rigorous requirements of the College and Career Readiness Standards (CCRS), the National Reporting System (NRS), and the Workforce Innovation and Opportunity Act (WIOA).

Adhering to the CASAS Math GOALS 2 test blueprint, the practice tests assess learners' understanding of the following math areas: *Number Sense and Operations, Consumer Economics, Algebraic Thinking, Geometry, Data Analysis and Statistics, and Pure Mathematics.*

More importantly, this resource increases learners' confidence, guides them to reflect on their learning and progress, and helps them transfer their knowledge to other contexts. Each practice test includes real-world activities that promote deep understanding and practical application of mathematical concepts. An answer key also accompanies each test.

By using this resource, you can save time, distribute practice sessions over several weeks, and assess and reinforce your learners' understanding of math functions and concepts. To order class sets, visit cbledu.com.

The CBL Team,

Your Partner in Student Learning

Dear Math Students,

This resource will help you develop and reinforce your math skills and test-taking ability. It will prepare you for the CASAS Math GOALS 2 Level E test. The practice tests will assess your understanding of the following math areas: *Number Sense and Operations, Consumer Economics, Algebraic Thinking, Geometry, Data Analysis and Statistics, and Pure Mathematics.*

Important Strategies:

Follow the strategies below to develop and reinforce your mathematical thinking skills and test-taking ability.

1. Study and master the four operations (addition, subtraction, multiplication, and division). Learn several strategies to compute and perform operations.

2. Study and master the multiplication table by reviewing it at least once daily (5 to 10 minutes).

3. Look up the meanings of math concepts (e.g., *sum, product, quotient, fraction, triangle*). Try to describe their meanings in your own words.

4. Seek to understand math ideas or the big picture before practicing the details or simple exercises. You can do that by using YouTube videos or Khan Academy.

5. Connect math ideas and concepts to real-world objects or situations. Ask your instructors for real-life examples.

6. Ask clarifying questions to ensure you understand everything before your class ends.

7. Practice solving word problems weekly (20-30 minutes) without distraction (TV, PC, cellphone, noise).

8. Solve math operations and problems on paper. Always show your work—including your strategies or reasoning—on paper.

9. Study and practice math in a group or with a classmate. Discuss your math solutions and strategies.

10. Explain math ideas and concepts to yourself or someone else orally. After doing this orally, you can also do it using drawings and writing.

11. Always reflect on your progress and strategies. After each practice session or test, identify what works well and why you make certain mistakes. Review and focus on practicing math ideas and concepts you don't understand well.

12. Celebrate your achievements. Any increase in math knowledge is an achievement.

Remember, math skills are essential for success in various aspects of your life, including community involvement, managing family finances, and professional advancement. By committing to completing the practice tests in this book, you'll be setting yourself up for success in your academic pursuits and beyond.

Let's get to work!

HOW TO APPROACH MATH WITH CONFIDENCE

Here are nine (9) practical ways you can overcome math fear and anxiety and build confidence while using this math book:

1. **Start Small:** Begin with easier problems that you can solve to build your confidence before solving harder ones.

2. **Use the book's Strategies:** Take advantage of this resource's strategies and practice tests. They are designed to help you understand, practice, and sharpen your math skills.

3. **Set Small Goals:** Break your math studies into small, achievable goals. Celebrate when you reach these goals to motivate yourself.

4. **Practice Regularly:** Consistent practice makes learning math more manageable. Try to work on math problems a few times a week.

5. **Take Breaks:** If you feel overwhelmed, take a short break. Come back to the math problems with a clear mind.

6. **Ask for Help:** Don't hesitate to seek help when you need it. Ask a teacher or a classmate, or use online resources if you're stuck.

7. **Stay Positive:** Keep a positive attitude about math. Remind yourself that you can handle it and that it's okay to make mistakes as you learn.

8. **Understand, Don't Memorize:** Focus on understanding the math ideas and concepts rather than just memorizing formulas. This understanding will make you feel more confident in solving math problems and taking math tests.

9. **Visualize Success:** Picture yourself successfully solving problems and understanding concepts. This visualization can boost your confidence.

By following these strategies, you will be able to study well and practice math with more confidence.

You have 80 minutes to answer 36 questions.

1. What is x in the following proportion?

$$\frac{1{,}296\ bags}{x} = \frac{72\ bags}{5\ minutes}$$

   A. 90 minutes

   B. 87 minutes

   C. 121 minutes

   D. 93 minutes

2. Cameron got 2 problems wrong for every 9 problems right on a math test. How many problems did Cameron get wrong if there were 55 problems altogether on the math test?

   A. 12

   B. 15

   C. 10

   D. 5

3. For every \$60 that Henry makes, he spends \$45. The rest goes into his savings account. If his weekly take-home pay is \$740, how much does he save each week?

   A. \$180

   B. \$185

   C. \$200

   D. \$170

4. Which of the following is an irrational number?

   A. $\sqrt{4} + \sqrt{9}$

   B. $\sqrt{7}$

   C. 0.345

   D. 2/7

5. Which of the following is **not** an irrational number?

   A. π

   B. $\sqrt{22}$

   C. $\sqrt[3]{3}$

   D. $\sqrt{81}$

6. Every minute, 2.5 gallons of water flow through a shower. A family of 5 people showers for an average of 6 minutes per person every morning. How many gallons of water does the family use for showering every morning?

A. 75 gallons

B. 60 gallons

C. 65 gallons

D. 70 gallons

Look at the following sale receipt:

7. How many items were purchased?

A. 6

B. 7

C. 8

D. 4

8. Which item was the cheapest?

A. Soda

B. Burger

C. Beer

D. Pizza slice

9. What is the cost of each soda?

A. $48

B. $12

C. $29

D. $9.67

10. What is the subtotal amount?

A. $105

B. $110

C. $103

D. $100

11. What is the total amount?

A. $105.06

B. $103.06

C. $100.94

D. $106.25

12.

In the cryptocurrency market,
1 Ethereum = $3,320.60.
What is the value of $1,000,000 in Ethereum?
(Round your answer to 2 decimals.)

A. 0.03 ETH

B. 148.70 ETH

C. 151.22 ETH

D. 301.15 ETH

13. Malcom's pool can hold a maximum of 4,530 gallons of water. The pool already contains 1,500 gallons of water. He begins to add more water at a rate of 30 gallons per minute. How many minutes can Malcom continue to add water without exceeding the maximum number of gallons?

A. 95 minutes

B. 88 minutes

C. 101 minutes

D. 110 minutes

14. Solve the following inequality:

$$0.15p + 12 \leq 15$$

A. $\square \geq 20$

B. $\square \leq 40$

C. $\square \geq 10$

D. $\square \leq 20$

15. Fifteen cups of coffee and 12 bagels cost $87. Eight cups of coffee and 20 bagels cost $108. What is the cost of each bagel?

A. $4.50

B. $3.00

C. $2.50

D. $4.00

16. Solve the following simultaneous linear equations:

$$4m + 5n = 68$$
$$m + n = 15$$

A. m = 7 and n = 8

B. m = 8 and n = 7

C. m = 6 and n = 9

D. m = 9 and n = 6

17. Let T(x) be the outside temperature (°F) x hours after 7 AM. What does the statement T(3) = 77 mean?

A. The outside temperature is 3°F, 77 hours after 7 AM.

B. The outside temperature is 77°F at 10 AM.

C. The outside temperature is 77°F at 7 AM.

D. After 77 hours, the outside temperature is 3°F.

18. Given f(x) = 0.75x + 6, what is f(4)?

A. 6

B. 4.50

C. 8.75

D. 9

19. The formula for converting degrees Celsius to degrees Kelvin is $F = 1.8K - 459.67$, where F is the temperature in degrees Fahrenheit and K is the temperature in degrees Kelvin. If the temperature is 280 degrees Fahrenheit, what is it in Kelvin?

A. 495.53 °K

B. 410.93 °K

C. 397.87 °K

D. 323.41 °K

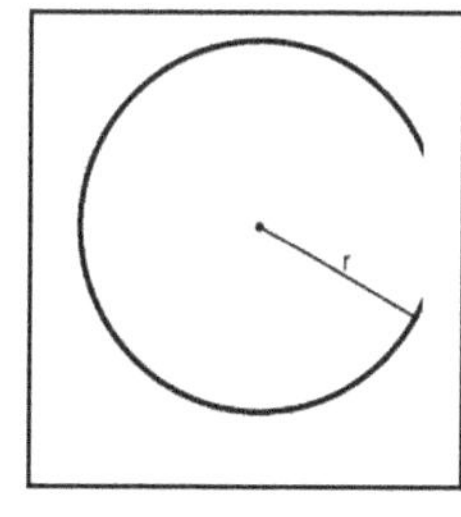

The formula for the area of the circle is
$$A = \pi r^2$$
A is the area of the circle and r is its radius.

20. What is the formula for the radius of the circle?

A. $r = \dfrac{2A}{\pi}$

B. $r = \dfrac{A}{2\pi}$

C. $r = \sqrt{\dfrac{A}{\pi}}$

D. $r = \sqrt{\dfrac{\pi}{A}}$

21. What is the volume of a sphere with a radius of 5 inches? (Use $\pi = 3.14$)

    A. 314.00 in^3 C. 518.31 in^3

    B. 212.44 in^3 D. 523.33 in^3

22. If the volume of a cube is 1,000 cubic inches, what is the length of each side?

    A. 20 inches   C. 100 inches

    B. 10 inches   D. 60 inches

23. What is the surface area of the following shape?

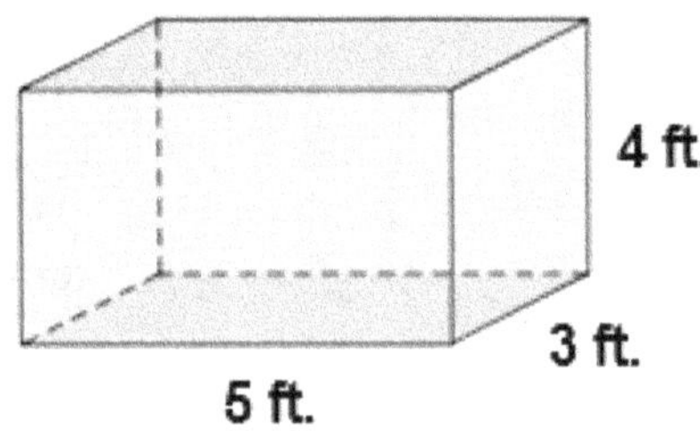

    A. 94 ft^2 C. 86 ft^2

    B. 64 ft^2 D. 98 ft^2

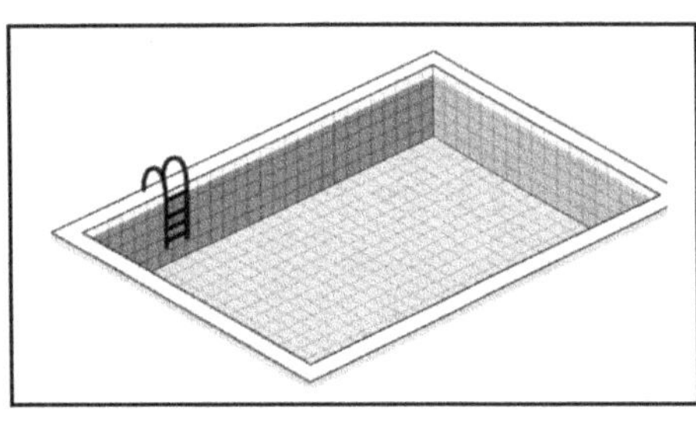

A swimming pool is 30 feet long, 16 feet wide and 8 feet deep. The water-resistant paint needed for the pool costs $2.50 per square foot.

24. What is the volume of the pool?

    A. 3,870 cubic feet   C. 3,590 cubic feet

    B. 3,650 cubic feet   D. 3,840 cubic feet

25. How much will it cost to paint the interior surfaces of the pool?

    A. $1,216   C. $3,040

    B. $1,520   D. $3,528

26.

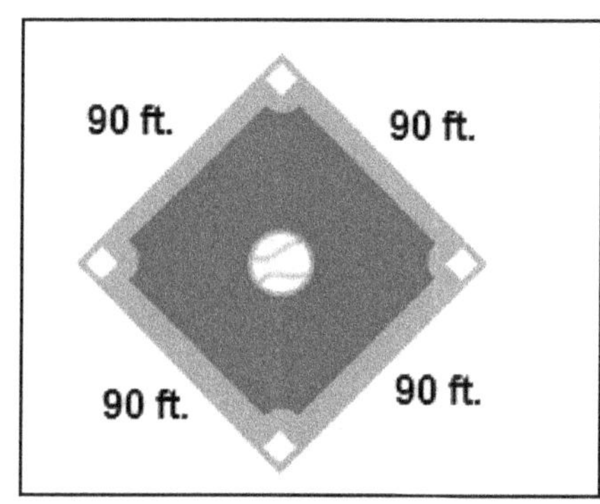

A baseball diamond is a square that is 90 feet on each side. What is the distance a player has to throw the ball from second base to home plate?

A. 180 ft.	C. 127.28 ft.
B. 130.50 ft.	D. 189.73 ft.

27. Rose leaves the house to go to school. She walks 24 yards west and 10 yards north. How far away is she from her starting point?

A. 34 yd.	C. 28 yd.
B. 26 yd.	D. 14 yd.

28. Which of the following shapes are congruent?

A. Shape 1 and Shape 3	C. Shape 2 and Shape 1
B. Shape 4 and Shape 2	D. All shapes are congruent.

29. The population density of a town is 234 people per square mile. If 35,100 people live in the town, how many square miles is the town?

A. 98 square miles	C. 144 square miles
B. 130 square miles	D. 150 square miles

30. There are 36 red cards and 44 blue cards in a box. If one card is chosen at random, what is the probability of getting a blue card?

A. 55%

B. 45%

C. 60%

D. 72%

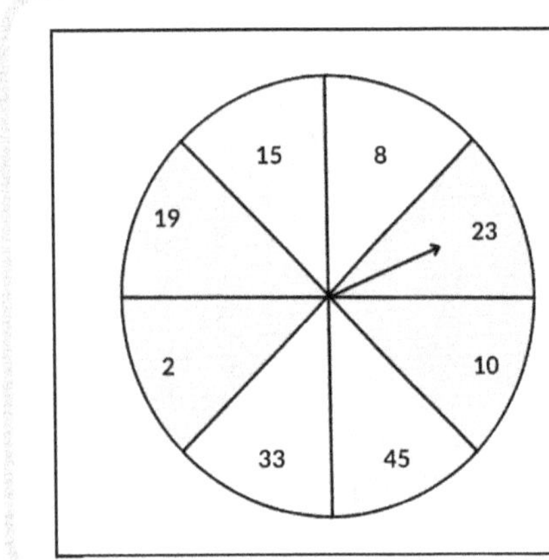

A spinner wheel has 8 equal sectors colored with some numbers.

31. What is the probability of the pointer landing on an odd number after spinning the wheel?

A. 0.550

B. 0.375

C. 0.555

D. 0.625

32. What is the probability of the pointer landing on a number less than 15 after a spin?

A. 0.375

B. 0.210

C. 0.255

D. 0.500

33. What is the probability of landing on a black sector after spinning the wheel?

A. 0.5

B. 0.1

C. 1

D. 0

34. What is the probability of landing on a white sector after spinning the wheel?

A. 0.50

B. 0.15

C. 0.25

D. 0.75

35. The grades obtained by a student in five math tests are 66, X, 81, 59, and 74. If the mean of the grades is 70, what is X?

A. 73

B. 80

C. 65

D. 70

36. What is the mode of the following data set: 2.05, 2.01, 2.04, 2.05, 2.03, 2.02, 2.30, 2.11, 2.05, and 2.05?

A. 2.01

B. 2.04

C. 2.11

D. 2.05

1) A	19) B
2) C	20) C
3) B	21) D
4) B	22) B
5) D	23) A
6) A	24) D
7) B	25) C
8) A	26) C
9) D	27) B
10) C	28) C
11) A	29) D
12) D	30) A
13) C	31) D
14) D	32) A
15) A	33) D
16) A	34) C
17) B	35) D
18) D	36) D

REFLECTION ON LEARNING

After completing Practice Test #1, reflect on your performance by answering the questions below. Discuss your responses with your instructor or a classmate.

1- What questions did you answer incorrectly? List the question numbers.

2- Review the list. What types of questions (operations, measurements, algebra, geometry, data analysis, statistics, graph, pie chart) did you answer incorrectly?

3- Review each question you've missed. Why do you think you answered the question incorrectly?

4- Based on the questions you missed, what math functions or concepts do you need to study and practice more? List them.

5- Review the question you got correctly. What strategies or methods did you use? What did you do well?

6- After reviewing all the questions, what questions do you have for your instructor?

You have 80 minutes to answer 36 questions.

1. A group of 24 students wrote essays in a class. Each student wrote 6 essays, and each essay contained an average of 1,250 words. How many words did the students write?

    A. 200,000 words

    B. 30,250 words

    C. 180,000 words

    D. 174,540 words

2. What is n in the following proportion?

$$\frac{3.4\ pounds}{\$1.50} = \frac{68\ pounds}{n}$$

    A. $30

    B. $26

    C. $15

    D. $28

3. Kenny can drive 405 miles on a tank of 30 gallons. How far can it drive on 60 gallons?

    A. 800 miles

    B. 810 miles

    C. 735 miles

    D. 794 miles

4. An ounce of sugar has about 110 calories. If a handful of sugar has 415 calories, what's the weight of the sugar in ounces?

    A. 0.27 ounces

    B. 45.65 ounces

    C. 5.34 ounces

    D. 3.77 ounces

5. If a = 5 and b = 2, which of the following is an irrational number?

    A. $\sqrt{b+2}$

    B. $\frac{a}{b}$

    C. $\sqrt{a}$

    D. $\sqrt{a+4}$

6. Which of the following is true?

    A. All radicals are irrational.

    B. All fractions are irrational.

    C. $\sqrt{11}$ is a radical.

    D. $\sqrt{7}$ is not irrational.

7. You hear in the news, "Tuition is expected to increase by 8.5% next year." If tuition this year was $1,400 per semester, what would it be next year?

   A. $1,476.50

   B. $1,519

   C. $1,520.25

   D. $1,190

> At a store, Cookies Delights costs $20 for a 12-pound bag, Nature's Cookies costs $25 for a 10-pound bag and Smart Cookies costs $14 for a 6-pound bag.

8. What is the unit price for Nature´s Cookies?

   A. $2.50 per pound

   B. $1.67 per pound

   C. $1.80 per pound

   D. $0.56 per pound

9. What is the cost of a 9-pound bag of Smart Cookies?

   A. $18

   B. $23

   C. $21

   D. $15

10. What is the better deal?

   A. Nature's Cookies

   B. Smart Cookies

   C. Delights Cookies

11. Maggie purchased a new printer for $1,050. If sales tax is 4.5%, what was the total of her purchase?

   A. $1,110

   B. $1,090.75

   C. $1,124

   D. $1,097.25

12. A pair of shoes originally costs $92, but there's a 15% discount on them. If the sales tax rate is 5% on the discounted price, how much will you pay in total, including tax, after the discount?

   A. $83

   B. $82.80

   C. $81

   D. $82.11

13. Solve the following inequality:

$$7y - 35 > 2y$$

   A. $\square > 5$

   B. $\square < 7$

   C. $\square > 6$

   D. $\square > 7$

14. There are 40 animals on a farm. Some are chickens and some are pigs. There are 124 legs in all. How many of each animal are there?

A. 22 pigs and 18 chickens

B. 18 pigs and 22 chickens

C. 23 pigs and 17 chickens

D. 15 pigs and 25 chickens

15. Solve the following simultaneous linear equations:

$$m + n = 67$$
$$3n - m = 1$$

A. m = 17 and n = 50

B. m = 50 and n = 17

C. m = 37 and n = 30

D. m = 22 and n = 45

16. It costs the class $30 to make cookies for the bake sale. How many cookies must they sell at 20 cents each to make a profit?

A. Less than 100 cookies

B. More than 150 cookies

C. Less than 150 cookies

D. At least 80 cookies

17. Given $f(t) = 5t^2 + 2t + 1$, what is $f(0) + f(2)$?

A. 32

B. 20

C. 26

D. 25

18. The function $A(m) = 50m + 630$ represents the amount of money in savings account A as a function of time in months, m. What does the statement A(5) mean?

A. The amount of money in the savings account after five months

B. The number of months

C. The amount of money in the savings account five months ago

D. Five times the amount of money in the savings account

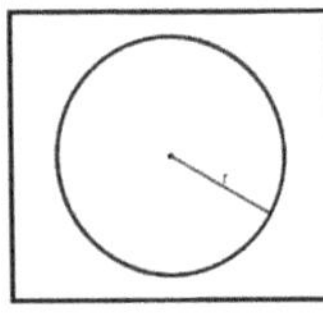

The formula for the circumference of the circle is
$$C = 2\pi r$$
Where C is the circumference of the circle and r is its radius.

19. What is the formula for the radius of the circumference?

A. $r = 2\pi C$

B. $r = \dfrac{2\pi}{C}$

C. $r = \dfrac{C}{2\pi}$

D. $r = \dfrac{\pi}{2C}$

20. What is the circumference of a circle with a radius of 4 inches? (Use $\pi = 3.14$)

    A. 26.32 inches   C. 12.56 inches

    B. 25.12 inches   D. 50.24 inches

21. If the circumference of a circle is $100\,\pi$ feet, what is the radius of the circumference?

    A. 50 feet   C. 75 feet

    B. 25 feet   D. 100 feet

22. A cylindrical water tank has a radius of 11 feet and a height of 17 feet. What is the maximum volume that the water tank can hold? (Use $\pi = 3.14$)

    A. 6,458.98 cubic inches   C. 3,195.62 cubic inches

    B. 6,582.74 cubic inches   D. 5,580.14 cubic inches

23. A cake decorator rolls a piece of stiff paper to form a cone. He cuts off the tip of the cone and uses it as a funnel to pour decorative sprinkles into containers. The cone has a radius of 6 inches and a height of 13 inches. What is the volume of the cone before the end is cut off? (Use $\pi = 3.14$)

    A. 485.51cubic inches   C. 495.29 cubic inches

    B. 489.84 cubic inches   D. 507.33 cubic inches

24. What is the surface area of a cube with a volume of 216 cubic feet?

    A. 36 ft^2 C. 216 ft^2

    B. 108 ft^2 D. 124 ft^2

25.

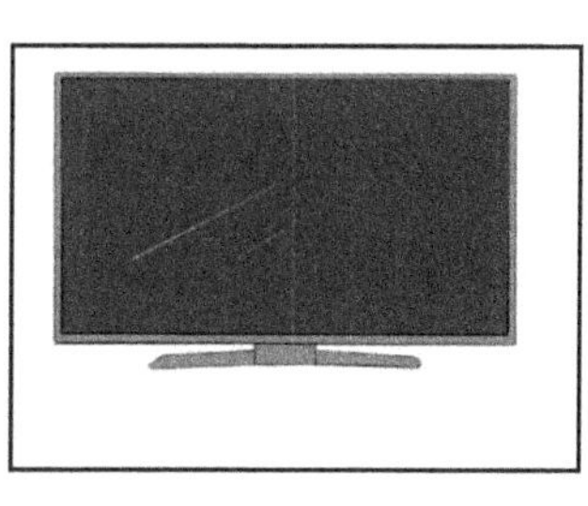

A store is selling 50-inch Smart TVs. This measurement is the **diagonal** distance across each screen. If a screen measures 44 inches in width, what is the actual height of the screen?

    A. 66.60 inches   C. 25 inches

    B. 23.75 inches   D. 21inches

26. David is building a slide for his kids. The ladder is 10 feet tall and the slide is 12.5 feet long. What is the distance between the base of the ladder and the bottom of the slide?

A. 7.5 feet

B. 16 feet

C. 12 feet

D. 9.5 feet

27. The following rectangles are similar. What is x?

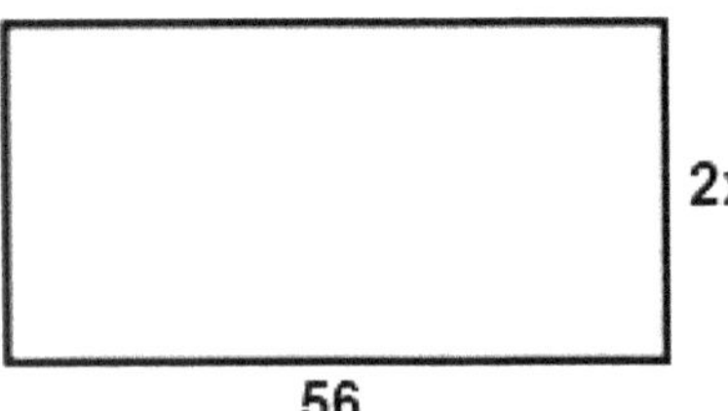

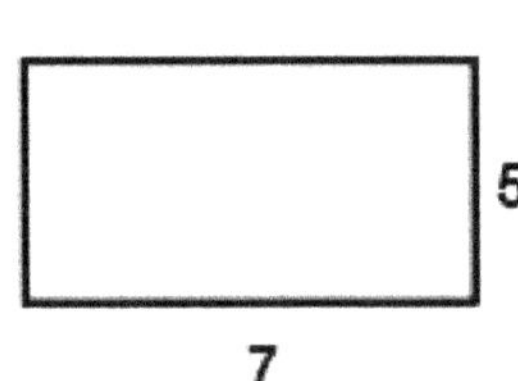

A. 40

B. 24

C. 20

D. 18

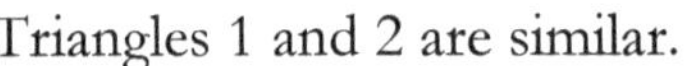

Triangles 1 and 2 are similar.

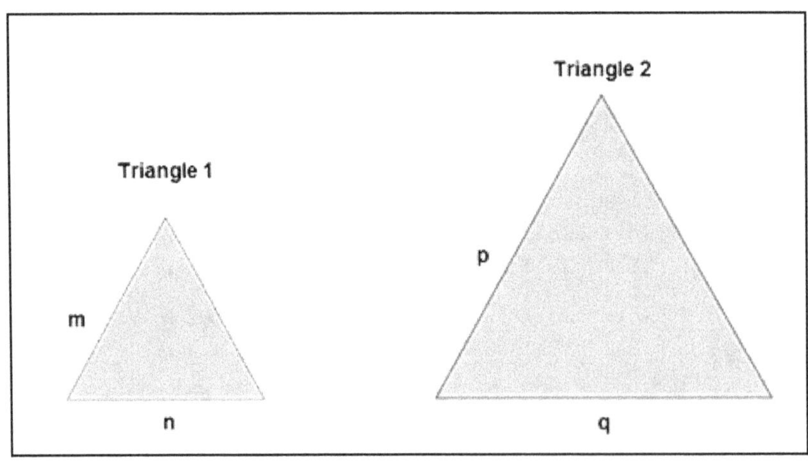

28. Which of the following is true?

A. $m + n = p + q$

B. $\dfrac{m}{q} = \dfrac{n}{p}$

C. $mn = pq$

D. $\dfrac{m}{p} = \dfrac{n}{q}$

29. If m = 3, n = 4, and q = 32, what is p?

A. 24

B. 12

C. 16

D. 28

30. Suppose that Triangle 1 and Triangle 2 are congruent. If the area of Triangle 2 is 37 square inches, what is the area of Triangle 1?

A. 14 square inches

B. 26 square inches

C. 37 square inches

D. Cannot be determined

31. Which of these numbers cannot be a probability?

A. 0.009%

B. 1.005

C. 2/87

D. 0.444

32. Julia writes each letter of the alphabet on a different slip of paper and puts the slips into a hat. What is the probability of randomly drawing one slip of paper from the hat and getting a consonant?

A. 5/26

B. 21/26

C. 2/13

D. 7/13

33. What is the probability of getting a number greater than 2 when a die is rolled?

A. 1/4

B. 1/6

C. 1/5

D. 2/3

The following two-way table shows the preference of cats or dogs in two groups:

Preference	Group A	Group B
Cats	72	y
Dogs	x	88
No preference	17	11
Total	144	142

34. What is x?

A. 55

B. 53

C. 48

D. 58

35. How many students prefer dogs?

A. 88

B. 140

C. 143

D. 152

36. What is y?

A. 43

B. 40

C. 38

D. 39

1)	C	19)	C
2)	A	20)	B
3)	B	21)	A
4)	D	22)	A
5)	C	23)	B
6)	C	24)	C
7)	B	25)	B
8)	A	26)	A
9)	C	27)	C
10)	C	28)	D
11)	D	29)	A
12)	D	30)	C
13)	D	31)	B
14)	A	32)	B
15)	B	33)	D
16)	B	34)	A
17)	C	35)	C
18)	A	36)	A

REFLECTION ON LEARNING

After completing Practice Test #2, reflect on your performance by answering the questions below. Discuss your responses with your instructor or a classmate.

1- What questions did you answer incorrectly? List the question numbers.

2- Review the list. What types of questions (operations, measurements, algebra, geometry, data analysis, statistics, graph, pie chart) did you answer incorrectly?

3- Review each question you've missed. Why do you think you answered the question incorrectly?

4- Based on the questions you missed, what math functions or concepts do you need to study and practice more? List them.

5- Review the question you got correctly. What strategies or methods did you use? What did you do well?

6- After reviewing all the questions, what questions do you have for your instructor?

You have 80 minutes to answer 36 questions.

1. A dog runs at a rate of 18 miles per hour. How far does he run in 40 minutes?

   A. 10 miles

   B. 12 miles

   C. 15 miles

   D. 19 miles

2. In a party, 22 drinks are required for every 14 people. If there are 266 people, how many drinks are required?

   A. 420

   B. 400

   C. 397

   D. 418

3. Albert has saved $230 in the past 20 days. At this rate, how much will he save in five weeks?

   A. $402.50

   B. $420

   C. $405.55

   D. $404

> Look at the following formula:
> $$T = \sqrt{5 \cdot m}$$

4. Let m = 2. Which of the following is true?

   A. T is a rational number.

   B. $T = \sqrt{52}$

   C. T is a fraction.

   D. $T = \sqrt{10}$

5. Let m = 5. Which of the following is true?

   A. T is an irrational number.

   B. T = 25

   C. $T = \sqrt{55}$

   D. T is a rational number.

6. Which value of m makes T = 25?

   A. 25

   B. 50

   C. 125

   D. 150

7. Which of the following is an irrational number?

A. 7.071

B. $\sqrt{49}$

C. $4 - \sqrt{4}$

D. $\sqrt{19}$

8. What is the value of 150 dollars in nickels? (Hint: 1 Nickel = 5 cents)

A. 850 nickels

B. 350 nickels

C. 3,000 nickels

D. 1,500 nickels

9. Zoe makes $785.50 each month. How much money will she make in 3 years and 3 months?

A. $30,634.50

B. $28,278.70

C. $30,860.55

D. $33,470.75

Look at the following gas bill.

▶Account Summary

Previous Amount Due on 05/05/2022	$87.99
Payments Received by 05/11/2022 Thank You	$0.00
Balance on 05/11/2022	$87.99
Charges for Gas Service This Period	+$31.23

Please Pay This Amount   **$119.22**

Amount Past Due - Pay Immediately   **$87.99**

Current Charges Due by 06/06/2022   **$31.23**

- For more information regarding these charges, see the Detail Charges section.

10. What is the total amount due?

A. $87.99

B. $119.22

C. $31.23

D. $56.76

11. If the gas bill increases by 3.5% for the next month, what will the total amount be?

A. $125.99

B. $124.46

C. $120.50

D. $123.39

12. The gas bill decreased by 5% for the previous month. What was the total amount due?

A. $113.26

B. $112.80

C. $113.45

D. $115.35

13. What is the inequality that represents Lisa's situation?

    A. $3.85 + 0.92m \leq 60$

    B. $3.85 - 0.92m \geq 60$

    C. $3.85 - 0.92\,m \leq 60$

    D. $3.85 + 0.92m < 60$

14. How many miles can Mary travel without exceeding her budget?

    A. 63 miles

    B. 68 miles

    C. 61 miles

    D. 71 miles

15. Suppose that the company charges \$5.20 as a flat rate. How many miles can Mary travel without exceeding her budget?

    A. 60 miles

    B. 63 miles

    C. 61 miles

    D. 59 miles

Look at the following pair of simultaneous equations:

$$P - Q = 40$$
$$P + Q = 100$$

16. What is the value of Q?

    A. 40

    B. 30

    C. 70

    D. 35

17. What is the value of 2P + 2Q?

    A. 100

    B. 120

    C. 200

    D. 160

18. Let $s = 8t^2 - 5$. What is the value of s when t = 3?

    A. 72

    B. 66

    C. 61

    D. 67

19. George's class had a math test where the grades were between 0 and 100. Let $N(x)$ represent the number of students whose grade on the exam was x. What does the statement $N(73) = 5$ mean?

A. There are 73 students whose grade on the exam was 5.

B. There are 5 students whose grade on the exam was 73.

C. The average grade of the class was 73.

D. The average grade of the class was 5.

20. If $f(x) = 14 - 6x$, what is $f(0) + f(1)$?

A. 20

B. 22

C. 14

D. 8

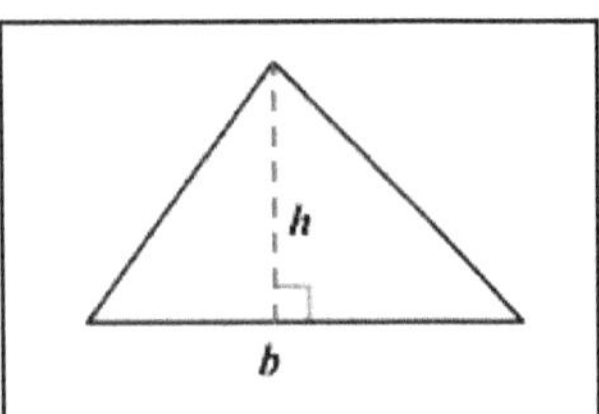

The formula for the area of a triangle is equal to half the product of its base and height.

$$A = \frac{b \cdot h}{2}$$

Where A is the area of the triangle, b is the base and h is its height.

21. What is the formula for the height of a triangle?

A. $h = \frac{2A}{b}$

B. $h = 2Ab$

C. $h = \frac{2b}{A}$

D. $h = 2A - b$

22. What is the formula for the base of a triangle?

A. $b = \frac{2h}{A}$

B. $b = 2Ah$

C. $b = \frac{A}{2h}$

D. $b = \frac{2A}{h}$

23. What is the area of a triangle whose height and base are 8 ft. and 11 ft., respectively?

A. 88 ft^2

B. 46 ft^2

C. 44 ft^2

D. 80 ft^2

24. What is the base of a triangle whose height and area are 10 ft. and 65 ft^2, respectively?

A. 13 ft.

B. 16 ft.

C. 26 ft.

D. 18 ft.

An **open** box in the shape of a cube
has a side length of 14 inches.

25. What is the volume of the box?

A. 1,176 in^3

B. 2,775 in^3

C. 2,670 in^3

D. 2,744 in^3

26. What is the surface area of the box?

A. 980 in^2

B. 1,150 in^2

C. 1,176 in^2

D. 1,200 in^2

27. If the side length of the box is 20 inches, what is the surface area?

A. 400 in^2

B. 1,200 in^2

C. 1,500 in^2

D. 2,000 in^2

28. Bret wants to replace the net on his basketball hoop. The hoop is 11 feet high. Bret places his ladder 6 feet from the base of the hoop. How long must the ladder be to reach the hoop?

A. 10.15 ft.

B. 12.53 ft.

C. 16.78 ft.

D. 11.96 ft.

Look at the triangle ABC on the coordinate plane:

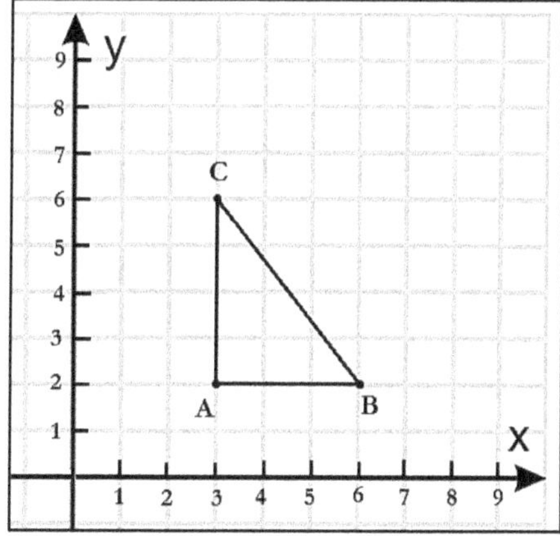

29. What is the length of side AC?

A. 6

B. 4

C. 7

D. 5

30. What is the length of side BC?

    A. 5   C. 7

    B. 5.5   D. 6

31. Dylan rolls a fair die with sides labeled K, P, E, L, A, and U. What is the probability that the die lands on a vowel?

    A. 16%   C. 20%

    B. 50%   D. 25%

The scores obtained by a student on six math tests are given below:

Test	1	2	3	4	5	6
Score obtained (points)	74	65	77	82	86	71

32. What is the probability of the student getting more than 80 points on a math test?

    A. 66.7%   C. 36.7%

    B. 35%   D. 33.3%

33. What is the mean of the scores?

    A. 74.43   C. 77.27

    B. 75.83   D. 76.22

34. What is the median of the scores?

    A. 75.5   C. 76

    B. 75   D. 76.5

35. What is the mode of the scores?

    A. 86   C. 82

    B. 74   D. There is no mode.

36. What is the range of the scores?

    A. 75   C. 21

    B. 86   D. 23

1) B	19) B
2) D	20) B
3) A	21) A
4) D	22) D
5) D	23) C
6) C	24) A
7) D	25) D
8) C	26) A
9) A	27) D
10) B	28) B
11) D	29) B
12) A	30) A
13) A	31) B
14) C	32) D
15) D	33) B
16) B	34) A
17) C	35) D
18) D	36) C

REFLECTION ON LEARNING

After completing Practice Test #3, reflect on your performance by answering the questions below. Discuss your responses with your instructor or a classmate.

1- What questions did you answer incorrectly? List the question numbers.

2- Review the list. What types of questions (operations, measurements, algebra, geometry, data analysis, statistics, graph, pie chart) did you answer incorrectly?

3- Review each question you've missed. Why do you think you answered the question incorrectly?

4- Based on the questions you missed, what math functions or concepts do you need to study and practice more? List them.

5- Review the question you got correctly. What strategies or methods did you use? What did you do well?

6- After reviewing all the questions, what questions do you have for your instructor?

You have 80 minutes to answer 36 questions.

1. If 5.75 pounds of meat serves 8 people, how many pounds will be needed to serve 48 people?

   A. 32.7 pounds

   B. 35.2 pounds

   C. 36 pounds

   D. 34.5 pounds

> The price of 5 T-shirts at Store 1 is $55. The price of 8 of the same T-shirts at Store 2 is $62. At Store 3, the price of a dozen of the same T-shirts is $120.

2. What is the cost of each T-shirt at Store 1?

   A. $10.00

   B. $11.00

   C. $9.50

   D. $8.50

3. What is the cost of each T-shirt at Store 3?

   A. $12.50

   B. $11.50

   C. $13

   D. $10

4. Which place offers the best deal?

   A. Store 2

   B. Store 1

   C. Store 3

5. Which of the following is true?

   A. $\sqrt{400} = 20$

   B. 0.012 is an irrational number.

   C. $\sqrt{144}$ is an irrational number.

   D. $\sqrt{2} = 1$

Look at the following sale receipt.

```
                GROCERY DEPOT
                   5000 GA-5
              Douglasville, GA 30135

              Cashier: ENZO G.

DELITE SKIM                    $10.36 TFA
  4EA      @ 2.59/EA
WHOLEMILK                       $7.77 TFA
  3EA      @ 2.59/EA
REDBULL                         $1.89 TFA
STRING CHEESE 16PK              $7.98 TFA
  2EA      @ 3.99/EA

SUBTOTAL            $28.00
TAX                 $1.82
TOTAL               $29.82
TEND                $29.82
CHANGE DUE          $0.00

              Item Count 10

              Thanks!!!


Date        Time     Lane Clerk Trans#
01/07/2019  09:45 AM  4    101  3854
```

6. How many items were purchased?

   A. 4

   B. 8

   C. 7

   D. 10

7. Which item was the most expensive?

   A. Delite Skim

   B. String Cheese

   C. Wholemilk

   D. Redbull

8. Which item was the cheapest?

   A. Redbull

   B. Delite Skim

   C. String Cheese

   D. Delite Skim

9. Suppose that the tax was 5%. What was the total amount?

   A. $30.22

   B. $31.10

   C. $29.40

   D. $30.40

10. What is the cost of a dozen Redbull?

   A. $23.40

   B. $22.43

   C. $20.90

   D. $22.68

11. Solve the following inequality.

$$8x + 25 < 10x$$

A. x < 12.5

B. x > 15

C. x > 12.5

D. x < 15

> Mildred buys 8 pretzels and 13 coffees in a shop and the cost is $89.
> Dennis buys 15 pretzels and 6 coffees in the same shop and they cost
> $63.
> Let x be the cost of each pretzel and y the cost of each coffee.

12. What are the simultaneous linear equations that represent this situation?

A. 13x + 8y = 63 and 6x + 15y = 89

B. 8x + 13y = 89 and 15x + 6y = 63

C. 6x + 8y = 63 and 13x + 15y = 89

D. 8x + 6y = 89 and 15x + 3y = 63

13. What is the cost of each pretzel?

A. $1.94

B. $3.50

C. $2.50

D. $2.00

14. What is the cost of each coffee?

A. $4.00

B. $4.50

C. $5.65

D. $6.25

> Laurie's coffee stand sells cups of coffee for $4.25 per cup. She spends $55
> on supplies. She can sell up to 80 cups with the supplies she has purchased.
> Let x be the number of cups of coffee and $f(x)$ be the profit in dollars.

15. Which function notation gives Laurie's profit?

A. $f(x) = 4.25x + 55$

B. $f(x) = 4.25x - 55$

C. $f(x) = 55x - 4.25$

D. $f(x) = 55x + 4.25$

16. What is Laurie's profit if she sells 38 cups of coffee?

A. $115.35

B. $107

C. $106.50

D. $105.95

17. What is her maximum profit?

A. $288

B. $270

C. $322

D. $285

18. If $f(x) = 8x^2 - 6x + 7$, what is $f(3)$?

A. 61

B. 63

C. 53

D. 44

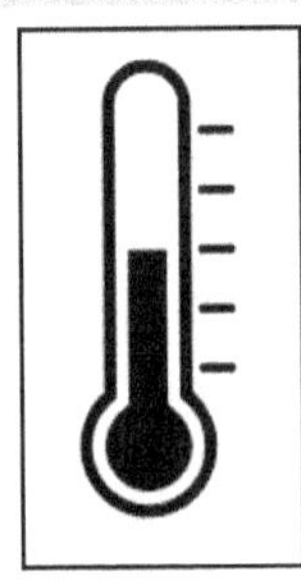

The temperature conversion formula from Celsius to Fahrenheit is:

$$°F = \frac{9}{5}°C + 32$$

C is the temperature in degrees Celsius (°C) and F is the temperature in degrees Fahrenheit (°F)

19. What is the temperature conversion formula from Fahrenheit to Celsius?

A. $°C = \frac{5}{9}°F - 32$

B. $°C = \frac{5}{9}°F + 32$

C. $°C = \frac{5}{9}(°F - 32)$

D. $C = \frac{9}{5}(°F - 32)$

20. The body temperature is generally 36°C. What is the body temperature in Fahrenheit degrees?

A. 99.6 °F

B. 94.6 °F

C. 82.6 °F

D. 96.8 °F

21. The boiling point of water is 100 °C. What is the boiling point of water in Fahrenheit degrees?

A. 222 °F

B. 212 °F

C. 200 °F

D. 312 °F

22. What is 0 °C in Fahrenheit?

A. − 32 °F

B. 32 °F

C. 64 °F

D. 0°F

23. For the formula $P = 5n^2$, what is the value of n when P = 45?

A. 3

B. 6

C. 9

D. 5

The radius of a soccer ball is 5 inches.
Use $\pi = 3.14$

24. What is the volume of the soccer ball?

A. 520.23 in^3

B. 467.96 in^3

C. 523.33 in^3

D. 500.12 in^3

25. What is the surface area of the soccer ball?

A. 312.96 in^2

B. 315.25 in^2

C. 314 in^2

D. 325.65 in^2

26. If the surface area of the soccer ball is 452.16 square inches, what is the radius of the soccer ball?

A. 7 inches

B. 4.5 inches

C. 5 inches

D. 6 inches

27. A swimming pool is 31 feet long, 22 feet wide and 8 feet deep. What is the volume of the pool?

A. 5,456 ft^3

B. 5,784 ft^3

C. 5,528 ft^3

D. 5,465 ft^3

28. In a right triangle, the length of the base is 7 inches, and the hypotenuse is 25 inches. What is the length of the missing side?

A. $\sqrt{32}$ in.

B. 32 in.

C. $\sqrt{74}$ in.

D. 24 in.

The following triangles are similar:

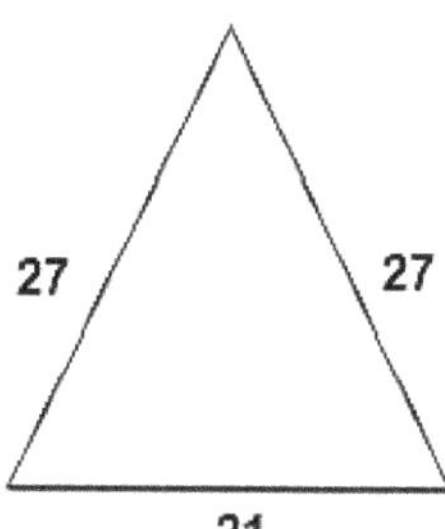

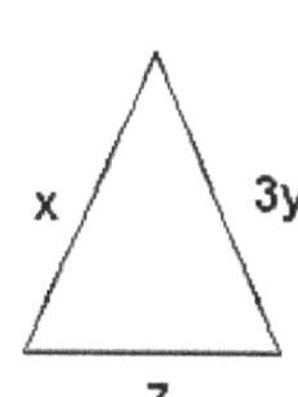

29. What is the value of x?

   A. 7   C. 9

   B. 6   D. 8

30. What is the value of y?

   A. 3   C. 9

   B. 6   D. 5

31. What is the value of x + 3y?

   A. 14   C. 12

   B. 18   D. 16

The following two-way table shows data on nationality and eye color.

	Brown or Hazel eyes	Blue or Green eyes	Total
English	91	19	110
Italian	28	42	**A**
German	33	15	48
Total	152	76	**B**

32. What is A?

   A. 70   C. 79

   B. 66   D. 72

33. What is B?

   A. 220   C. 228

   B. 207   D. 205

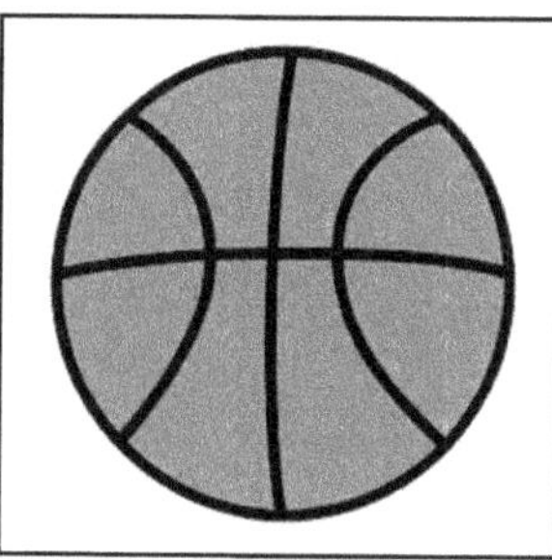

The following data show the number of points scored
by a basketball team over its last 9 games:
63, 89, 88, 73, 71, X, 82, 81, 94
The mean of the scores is 81.3.

34. What is *X*?

    A. 91   C. 101

    B. 82   D. 87

35. What is the median of the scores?

    A. 71   C. 82

    B. 83   D. 85

36. What is the range of the scores?

    A. 34   C. 37

    B. 31   D. 29

1) D	19) C
2) B	20) D
3) D	21) B
4) A	22) B
5) A	23) A
6) D	24) C
7) B	25) C
8) A	26) D
9) C	27) A
10) D	28) D
11) C	29) C
12) B	30) A
13) A	31) B
14) C	32) A
15) B	33) C
16) C	34) A
17) D	35) C
18) A	36) B

REFLECTION ON LEARNING

After completing Practice Test #4, reflect on your performance by answering the questions below. Discuss your responses with your instructor or a classmate.

1- What questions did you answer incorrectly? List the question numbers.

2- Review the list. What types of questions (operations, measurements, algebra, geometry, data analysis, statistics, graph, pie chart) did you answer incorrectly?

3- Review each question you've missed. Why do you think you answered the question incorrectly?

4- Based on the questions you missed, what math functions or concepts do you need to study and practice more? List them.

5- Review the question you got correctly. What strategies or methods did you use? What did you do well?

6- After reviewing all the questions, what questions do you have for your instructor?

ADULT ED
MATH
NUMBER SYSTEM, NUMBER SENSE, AND OPERATIONS PREPARING
FOR
CASAS, TABE 11 & 12, HISET, AND GED TESTING
BY COACHING FOR BETTER LEARNING

ADULT ED
MATH
GEOMETRY PREPARING
FOR
CASAS, TABE 11 & 12, HISET, AND GED TESTING
BY COACHING FOR BETTER LEARNING

CBL COACHING
Math
Practice Worksheets and Workbook for Adult Students
A learner-centered tool designed to help students practice and master the four operations while preparing them for CASAS Math GOALS 2, TABE 11 and 12, ACT, HiSET, GED tests, and IET programs.

SKILLS FOR SUCCESS IN CAREER AND TECHNICAL EDUCATION (CTE)
STUDENT GUIDE
A SYSTEMATIC WAY TO MASTER ORGANIZATIONAL AND SOFT SKILLS
CBL COACHING

HOW TO ACHIEVE BETTER STUDENT RETENTION IN ADULT EDUCATION
Secrets to becoming an indispensable adult-ed teacher that provides a learning experience that's hard to walk away from (and keeps administrators happy)
TEDDY EDOUARD

TABE 11 & 12
CONSUMABLE STUDENT READING MANUAL FOR LEVEL E
Preparing Adult Learners for TABE 11 & 12 Reading Tests and for Vocational Training and College Entrance Reading Exams
By Coaching for Better Learning, LLC

TABE 11 & 12
CONSUMABLE STUDENT READING MANUAL FOR LEVEL M
Preparing Adult Learners for TABE 11 & 12 Reading Tests and for Vocational Training and College Entrance Reading Exams
By Coaching for Better Learning, LLC

TABE 11 & 12
CONSUMABLE STUDENT READING MANUAL FOR LEVEL D
Preparing Adult Learners for TABE 11 & 12 Reading Tests and for Vocational Training and College Entrance Reading Exams
By Coaching for Better Learning, LLC

TABE 11 & 12
STUDENT LANGUAGE MANUAL FOR LEVEL E
Preparing Adult Learners for TABE 11 & 12 Language Tests and for Vocational Training and College Entrance Exams
By Coaching for Better Learning, LLC

TABE 11 & 12
STUDENT LANGUAGE MANUAL FOR LEVEL M
Preparing Adult Learners for TABE 11 & 12 Language Tests and for Vocational Training and College Entrance Exams
By Coaching for Better Learning, LLC

Preparing Adult Learners for TABE 11 & 12 Math Tests and for Vocational Training Entrance Math Exams
TABE 11 & 12
Consumable Student Math Workbook
FOR LEVEL E
By Coaching for Better Learning, LLC

Preparing Adult Learners for TABE 11 & 12 Math Tests and for Vocational Training Entrance Math Exams
TABE 11 & 12
Consumable Student Math Workbook
FOR LEVEL M
By Coaching for Better Learning, LLC

Preparing Adult Learners for TABE 11 & 12 Math Tests and for Vocational Training Entrance Math Exams
TABE 11 & 12
Consumable Student Math Workbook
FOR LEVEL D
By Coaching for Better Learning, LLC

Preparing Adult Learners for TABE 11 & 12 Math Tests and for Vocational Training Entrance Math Exams
TABE 11 & 12
Consumable Student Math Workbook
FOR LEVEL A
By Coaching for Better Learning, LLC

CBL COACHING
Workbook
Number and Letter Tracing for Adult Students
This tool is designed to help adult students practice and master handwriting. It is appropriate for literacy, ESL, and ABE classes.

READING NOTEBOOK & JOURNAL
For Adult Students
By Coaching For Better Learning   CBL COACHING

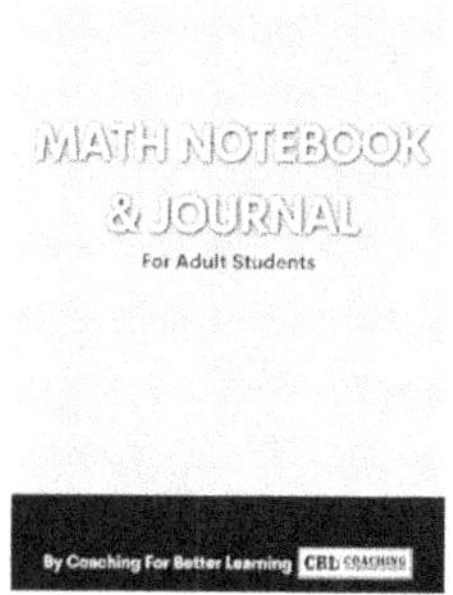

MATH NOTEBOOK & JOURNAL
For Adult Students
By Coaching For Better Learning   CBL COACHING

BOOK 1
PHONICS AND LIFE SKILLS READING
FOR
Adult Literacy, ABE, and ESL Students
Turning Learners into Proficient Readers
CBL COACHING

BOOK 2
PHONICS AND LIFE SKILLS READING
FOR
Adult Literacy, ABE, and ESL Students
Turning Learners into Proficient Readers
CBL COACHING

BOOK 3
PHONICS AND LIFE SKILLS READING
FOR
Adult Literacy, ABE, and ESL Students
Turning Learners into Proficient Readers
CBL COACHING

CBL equips programs and instructors to increase student retention, learning—and success.

We do it by offering evidence-based systematic solutions, learner-centered teaching materials, instructor-centered training, and future-oriented strategies in adult education, workforce development, and vocational training.

We teach proven insights, knowledge, and skills that are useful to practitioners (instructors, administrators, and support staff).

CBL also takes pride in publishing student-centered textbooks designed to prepare learners for CASAS, TABE 11&12, HiSET, and GED assessments and assist instructors in covering course curricula and standards with confidence.

Our publications also include teaching guides, test prep tools, and study guides that foster reflective learning, ensuring sustained engagement in active learning. Find our meticulously crafted textbooks on our book page (cbledu.com) or major platforms like Amazon, Barnes & Noble, and Ingram Spark.

CBL also guides adult education and workforce programs in establishing robust professional development programs—training, peer-mentoring, coaching, community of practices (CoPs), and instructional systems— fostering a culture of continuous improvement and contributing to higher learner retention and success rates. We also offer workshops and PD sessions for adult educators and classroom instructors.

If you have suggestions or questions about instructional systems, textbooks, or student learning and retention, contact us today at teamcbl@cbledu.com or 410-960-4082.